MARY
LOU
RETTON
AND
THE
NEW
GYMNASTS

MARY LOU RETTON

AND THE NEW GYMNASTS

BY HERMA SILVERSTEIN

A GROLIER COMPANY

FRANKLIN WATTS
NEW YORK • LONDON • TORONTO
SYDNEY • 1985

Cover photographs courtesy of UPI/Bettmann Newsphotos
Back cover photographs courtesy of: Rancinan/Guichard/Sygma

Photographs courtesy of:
Jerry Cooke/Sports Illustrated: pp. 1, 38;
Andy Hayt/Sports Illustrated: pp. 17, 24, 35, 57;
Walter Iooss, Fuji Film/Sports Illustrated: pp. 23, 54;
Peter Read Miller/Sports Illustrated: p. 27;
Brian Lanker/Sports Illustrated: p. 77;
AP/Wide World: pp. 4, 10, 13, 14, 41, 49;
UPI/Bettmann Newsphotos: pp. 7, 20, 29, 32, 58, 61;
Rancinan/Guichard/Sygma: p. 45; Alain Dejean/Sygma: p. 50;
Sutton/Sygma: p. 67; J.P. Laffont/Sygma: p. 68;
Focus on Sports: pp. 53, 65; Gary Gunderson: p. 71;
Michael Cates: p. 74.

Library of Congress Cataloging in Publication Data

Silverstein, Herma.
Mary Lou Retton and the new gymnasts.

Includes index.
Summary: Describes the styles, techniques, and accomplishments of the new Olympic gymnasts, with an emphasis
on Mary Lou Retton.
1. Gymnasts—Bibliography—Juvenile literature.
2. Gymnasts—United States—Biography—Juvenile literature.
3. Retton, Mary Lou, 1968–   —Juvenile literature.
4. Olympic games—Juvenile literature. 5. Gymnasts—
Juvenile literature. [1. Gymnasts. 3. Gymnastics.
3. Retton, Mary Lou, 1968–   . 4. Olympic games]
I. Title.
GV460.S55 1985   796.4′1′0922 [B] [920]   85-11471
ISBN 0-531-10053-7

CONTENTS

I DEDICATE THIS BOOK
WITH MY MOST SPECIAL LOVE
TO MAUREEN GORDON,
WHO PUT ME ON THE BEAM,
AND WHO HAS ALWAYS
BEEN THERE TO SPOT ME.

Acknowledgments

I wish to thank Michael Cates
of Broadway Gymnastics,
Santa Monica, California, for
his invaluable assistance in
providing me with technical
information about gymnastics,
and for his time and interest
in answering my many questions.

I especially thank Caroline Arnold,
for sharing her gifted expertise
with me, and for her meticulous
review of this manuscript,
in spite of persistent beckoning
from her own typewriter . . .

and Frank Sloan, for giving me
Mary Lou, and a chance to score
"a perfect ten."

MARY
LOU
RETTON
AND
THE
NEW
GYMNASTS

1

MEET MARY LOU RETTON

The petite gymnast with the pixie haircut concentrated on the vaulting horse at the end of the 80-foot (24-m) runway. She had to score a perfect ten on her vault to win the gold medal. A fraction less and she would tie Ecaterina Szabo for first place.

The gymnast shook her arms and legs, loosening her muscles. Then she blew her bangs off her forehead and jogged in place, trying to calm her fluttering heart. She *would* nail her vault. She did not want to tie. She wanted to win.

The occasion was the 1984 Olympics in Los Angeles, California, and the event was the finals of the women's individual all-around competition. The petite gymnast was Mary Lou Retton, and she was going for the gold.

Mary Lou squared her shoulders in determination and narrowed her saucer-sized brown eyes. Her pulse revved like a racing car as the judges flashed a green light, signaling her to begin. A tense silence fell over the arena.

Her raised arm said she was ready, then Mary Lou Retton exploded down the runway, hitting the springboard at the end like a jackhammer. She twisted into a handstand over the vault, her fingers barely brushing the leather as she launched into a full twist . . . a layout back somersault . . . and still soaring into a half-twist . . . a half-somersault . . . and *another* half-twist before . . . .

Whap! Her feet plowed into the mat. Mary Lou shot her arms up in victory, and let a gold medal grin dance across her face.

The audience roared with excitement, stamping their feet and pounding their hands. The judges did not need to

flash Mary Lou's score on the board. She knew what the number would be, as did everyone else in Pauley Pavilion, the sports arena on the UCLA campus where gymnastic meets are held.

Mary Lou Retton had nailed her pefect ten. She had beaten Romania's Ecaterina Szabo by .05 of a point and won the gold medal in the women's all-around competition, marking Mary Lou as the best woman gymnast in the world. She also became the first American gymnast, man or woman, to win the all-around championship in Olympic history.

Although gymnasts are allowed two turns on the vault, by scoring a ten on her first vault Mary Lou had no reason to take another turn. However, before her teammates could offer their congratulations, Mary Lou had sprinted back up the runway, signaled the judges she was ready, and given an instant replay of her perfect ten vault.

"Olympic champion!" shouted Bela Karolyi, her private coach and the former trainer of famous Romanian gymnast Nadia Comaneci. "I guarantee no gymnast in the world could have done what Mary Lou has. Nadia was a great champion, but Mary Lou is bigger . . . that strong a personality is fantastic, unbelievable."

Don Peters, coach of the United States women's Olympic gymnastic team, agreed: "You have to give it a ten. It's the best vault I've ever seen."

Mary Lou's vaulting routine, which she invented, and in which she flies a record 14 feet (4.2 m), is now named the "Retton Vault," and will be written about in sports books, along with the famous stunts of other gymnasts. One of the most popular of these stunts is a layout somersault (legs straight), with a full twist. It was invented by a Japanese gymnast, Mitsuo Tsukahara, and named the "Tsukahara," or the "Sook" for short, after him. In her Retton Vault, Mary Lou took the Tsukahara and added another full twist, a stunt no other gymnast would dare.

After a perfect vault, a jubilant Mary Lou knows the gold medal belongs to her.

Then, figuring if one is good, two are better, Mary Lou invented another original stunt, this one on the uneven parallel bars, now named the "Retton Flip" or "Retton Salto." "I do a giant swing into a handstand on the high bar," she explains her stunt, "and then I swoop down and belly-beat the low bar—Blam! And then I just swing back up, let go, and do a front somersault in the pike position [legs perpendicular to body], and land sitting on the high bar again." She raises her arms as if to say, "Look, everyone! No hands!"

At 4 feet 9 inches (1 m 46 cm) tall, and 95 pounds (35.5 k), Mary Lou Retton may seem small. However, she was born with a king-size portion of power and strength. Bela Karolyi says Mary Lou typifies the new gymnast in her raw nerve, extraordinary self-confidence, and bold aggression on the apparatus. Sports critics have called her charging runs and leaps upon the equipment "attacking the apparatus." Bela Karolyi describes Mary Lou's performances his own way: "She's so powerful physically, and she's mentally powerful, too. I was teaching gymnastics twenty-five years, and had many world and Olympic champions. But I never had somebody more positive and dedicated than this little girl. She's a little flyer . . . not a little flower."

No other gymnast can equal Mary Lou's rocket-speed leaps into hyperspace, or breathtaking body contortions. Totally fearless, she is the only known gymnast to begin her floor exercises with a double somersault in the layout position on the first pass, followed by two more double tuck somersaults (legs bent to chest), on the second and third passes. After each stunt, Mary Lou grins at the audience, communicating her sheer joy in accomplishment.

Her self-confidence shone through when she spoke of her strongest opponent in the 1984 Olympics, Ecaterina Szabo. "I've seen her perform, and she's terrific. But what she doesn't know about me is that I'm tougher than she is."

Coach Bela Karolyi
hugs his star pupil.

Just how tough was put to the test six weeks before the Los Angeles Games, when Mary Lou injured her right knee, causing cartilage fragments to slip underneath the bone. "My leg wouldn't work right," she recalls. "And I thought, 'It's all over for me.' But I was flown to Richmond, Virginia, for arthroscopic surgery, where they snick out some of the cartilages." Her doctors said her knee would not heal in time for the 1984 Olympics. "But I was back in the gym the next day," Mary Lou boasts. "No way was I going to miss the Olympics."

Bela Karolyi praises Mary Lou's endurance and determination, other features of the new gymnasts, by saying, "She never has to be pushed. If I ask her to try something one more time, she never says, 'I'm too tired,' or 'I'm having a bad day.' Never ever. It's always, 'Yes, let's go!' " Mary Lou seems to drive herself to practice gymnastics with the determination of a tiger stalking its prey. After her operation, she constantly chanted, "I'm gonna make it!"

The proof was in the vault. In addition to her gold medal, she and her teammates won a silver medal for their second-place finish in the team competition. This was the first medal ever won by an American women's gymnastic team in international competition. In addition, Mary Lou won another silver medal for her performance on the vault in the individual events competition, and two bronze medals for her routines on the uneven parallel bars and the floor exercises.

While the new gymnasts strive to perform well under the intense stress of international meets, Mary Lou Retton has the rare mental strength to perform her *best* under the pressure-cooker competition written about in hero stories. If Mary Lou, instead of Casey Jones, had been at bat in Mudville that day, Mary Lou Retton would never have struck out. When she needed that perfect ten to beat Ecaterina Szabo, she did not allow the narrow gap between their scores to distract her total concentration or hinder her excellent performance.

Later she said, "I knew by my takeoff that I had it. I knew by my vault that I had it. I knew it when I was in the *air*! Nobody thought it could be done. But you know what? I went and *did* it."

Don Peters says, "She thrives on pressure. She never gets uptight . . . A Great Champion."

Outside the gym, Mary Lou is a typical sixteen-year-old. She can't wait to get her driver's license, although her father says, "She'll have to sit on a cushion; she can't even reach the gas pedal."

When Mary Lou and teammate Julianne McNamara had some free time between gymnastic events at the Los Angeles Games, they went sightseeing. In their casual clothes they appeared like any teen-agers out for a day of fun. They shared pizza, gossiped about the Games, and looked for movie stars . . . especially for Mary Lou's idol at the time, Matt Dillon. As for dating, however, Mary Lou's seven-day training week leaves little time left over for any social life. "No time for boyfriends now," she says. "Boys can wait . . . but not too long."

Mary Lou Retton, world champion gymnast, becomes Mary Lou, teenager, when she visits her family in Fairmont, West Virginia, where she was born in 1968. Her hometown gave her a "Welcome Home" parade after the 1984 Olympics, and citizens lined the streets to get a glimpse of her. She smiled and waved with the professional poise of a Miss America as she rode through town in a convertible.

Yet after the parade she went home and turned into Mary Lou Retton, youngest member of the Retton family. Some of her gymnastic talent might have been inherited from her athletic family. Mary Lou's three older brothers are competitive athletes in baseball, basketball, and football. Her older sister, Shari, is a former gymnastic champion.

One wall of Mary Lou's room is covered with gymnastic ribbons. The other, however, in her "just Mary Lou" image, bears a cast from a wrist injury. The cast is autographed by her sports idol, Sugar Ray Leonard. Her closet is crammed with mementos, including her stuffed lamb collection. When she moved to Houston, Texas, to train with Bela Karolyi, she took her favorite lamb—a tattered animal whose ear she used to chew on when she was a baby.

Mary Lou Retton has come a long way from her first acrobatic performance at age four, when her mother nicknamed her "The Great Table Smasher and Lamp Toppler." Mrs. Retton remembers how Mary Lou "ran around the living room doing tumbling . . . bouncing off the walls and breaking up the furniture. I finally sent her off to dancing school . . . tap and ballet and acrobatics. It was the acrobatics that did it for Mary Lou."

(9)

Mary Lou responds, saying, "I was one of those hyper kids. Always jumping up and down on the couch and breaking things." Gymnastics provided her with an outlet for that energy. Her mother says that Mary Lou could outrun any boy on the block, and had the speed and strength, even as a child, of a flyweight boxer. She was fearless. Today her hyperactive energy is one of her assets as a gymnast, for she can practice for hours without tiring.

When Mary Lou was seven she stopped taking dancing lessons and took only gymnastics. She remembers lying on the living room rug watching the 1976 Olympics on television. When Nadia Comaneci scored the first perfect ten in Olympic history, Mary Lou exclaimed, "Oh my gosh! She's so wonderful!" Today Mary Lou asks, "Who would have thought?" For Mary Lou is now a gold medalist and an idol to young gymnasts herself.

Mary Lou attended gymnastics class once a week at that time, but she improved so rapidly that when a gymnastics club opened in Fairmont, she joined "to see if I could keep improving." By the time she was fourteen, Mary Lou had her answer. She qualified as an Elite gymnast, the top ranked level in gymnastics. All she needed now was to find the right coach to help perfect her talent.

During a gymnastics meet in Salt Lake City, Utah, Mary Lou met Bela Karolyi. It was "like at first sight." She begged him to train her at his gymnastic school in Houston and he agreed. However, Mary Lou's parents felt she was too young to leave home. "We held her back a year," Mrs. Retton said. "But we just knew that she'd gone as far as she could go here. After meets she'd come home crying, 'But, Mom, I could be the best.' "

When Mary Lou finally packed her bags for Houston, she and her parents drove twenty-four hours to Karolyi's

*Thousands of fans
turned out to greet
Mary Lou on her
arrival at the Houston
Intercontinental Airport.*

World Gymnastics, Incorporated. "It was Christmas time," Mary Lou remembers. "Leaving home was so hard. But if I hadn't gone, I would never be where I am today."

In March 1983 Mary Lou made her debut in international gymnastics. Her teammate on the United States women's Olympic gymnastic team, Dianne Durham, was injured shortly before the McDonald's American Cup Meet. This meet is considered the most prestigious of the international gymnastic competitions held in the United States. Mary Lou went on as an alternate at Madison Square Garden in New York City, where the McDonald's Cup is held.

By the time the meet ended, Mary Lou Retton had become a household name. She had won the individual events championship on the vault and floor exercises, tied for first place on the uneven parallel bars, and walked away wearing the women's all-around gold medal. She beat Natalia Yurchenko, the Soviet Union's all-around champion until this meet, as well as Boriana Stoyanova, Bulgaria's world vault champion until Mary Lou stole the title from her.

A year later at the 1984 McDonald's Cup Meet, Mary Lou gave a repeat performance of her 1983 triumphs, scoring a 39.50 out of a possible 40.

"Isn't this a kick?" Mary Lou says as she grins her famous ear-to-ear smile. "And to think it used to be so scary. There was a time when I wouldn't have believed it. But if you work hard, somehow it finally pays off. It becomes like fun."

When asked for her advice to aspiring gymnasts, Mary Lou replies, "It's all in the training. I work at this seven days a week—two long, hard practice sessions a day, drilling myself, going over everything again and again. Constantly."

Mary Lou dances on the balance beam at the 1984 McDonald's American Cup tournament, where she won the women's all-around gold medal for the second year in a row.

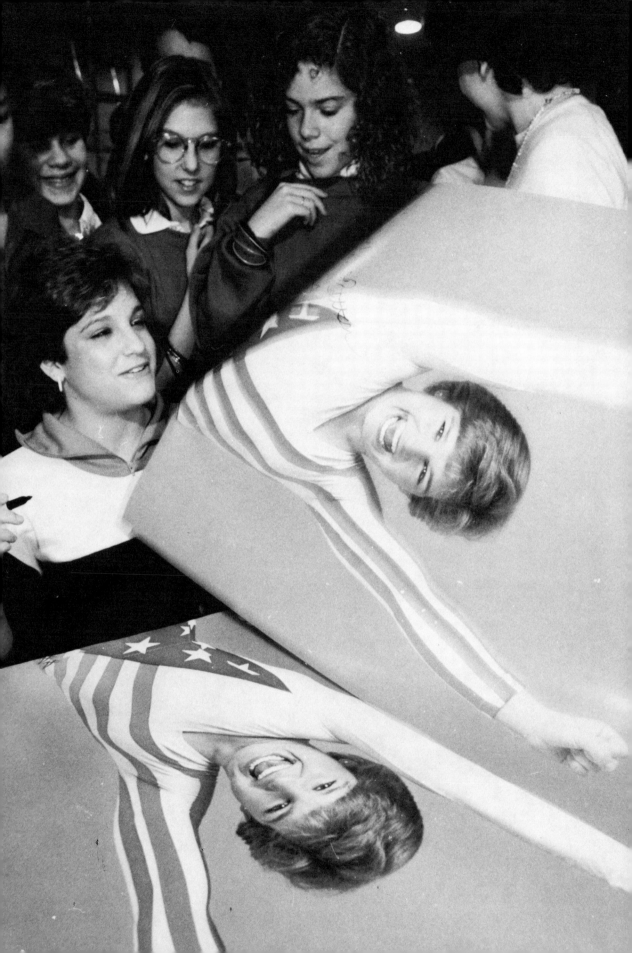

For the future, Mary Lou plans to keep training with Bela Karolyi. As the female world champion gymnast, there is little doubt that she will return to star in another Olympics. When she does, she most likely will have another original, awesome stunt inside her duffel bag to thrill spectators and to impress judges once again.

Mary Lou Retton is a *total* new gymnast. She has the dedication to the sport, the self-confidence to try new, risky stunts, and the power, flexibility, and endurance to master them. And perhaps most important, she expects to succeed. As she said, "I want to win."

Besides Mary Lou's incredible gymnastic skills, her bubbly personality and charm have captured the hearts of millions the world over. In December 1984 Mary Lou received another award to add to her growing collection. She was named sportswoman of the year by *Sports Illustrated* magazine. And in March 1985 Mary Lou became the first woman gymnast to win three American Cup all-around championships.

Even when she is performing her most difficult stunt, the love she has for gymnastics shines through in her sparkling eyes and joyful expresson. Concerning her gravity-defying routines, Mary Lou says, "I flat *love* flying like that!"

As she boarded the plane leaving Los Angeles after the 1984 Olympics, Mary Lou held up five medals, plus one extra souvenir of her gymnastic triumphs. Her contagious smile spread across her face as she exclaimed, "I am *never* going to wash this uniform!"

Mary Lou autographs posters of her photo that now adorns Wheaties cereal boxes. The occasion was a breakfast ceremony at a New York City school where Wheaties donated $50,000 to the United States Gymnastics Federation's Junior National Program.

2

MEET
THE
UNITED
STATES
MEN'S
GYMNASTIC
TEAM

Their daily ritual was a secret . . . a private Olympic fantasy, originated in college, and shared only between the two men.

After each gymnastic practice, Peter Vidmar and Tim Daggett waited until their teammates on the UCLA gymnastic team had left the gymnasium. "We'd turn off the radio," Peter said, "and the gym would be all silent. We'd go to the high bar and then we'd say, 'O.K., we have to hit both of our routines perfect in order to win the Olympic gold medal.' "

Peter and Tim would spin through their horizontal bar routines as if they were performing at the real Olympics. Peter remembers how "we'd always laugh, because it seemed so unrealistic. And all of a sudden we found ourselves in that exact situation. It was incredible."

The situation Peter referred to was the 1984 Olympics, when he and Tim made the United States men's Olympic gymnastic team. Peter and Tim's Olympic fantasy had come true. Their skilled acrobatics, along with the spectacular performances of fellow teammates Mitch Gaylord, Bart Conner, Scott Johnson, and James Hartung, scored high enough points to win America's first gold medal for team competition in Olympic history.

PETER
VIDMAR

The only married man on the team, Peter, twenty-three, was born in Los Angeles, and now makes his home in Santa Monica, California. He graduated from UCLA in 1983 with a degree in economics. That same year, Peter won the men's all-around championship in the American Cup Competition, an annual international gymnastics

meet. At the Los Angeles Games, Peter took second place in the men's all-around competition, losing to Japan's Koji Gushiken by a mere .025 of a point. His silver medal set a historic record as the first medal won by an American in the all-around competition in fifty-two years of Olympic Games. Peter won another individual gold medal when he tied with China's Li Ning for first place on the pommel horse competition.

A member of the U.S. men's gymnastic team for seven years, Peter began his training in 1972. His teammates call him "The Serious Gymnast" as he is the most self-disciplined man on the team. James Hartung says, "Peter is the kind of guy you look up to. He just does everything right. . . ."

TIM DAGGETT   Another UCLA student is Tim Daggett, twenty-two, from Springfield, Massachusetts. His major is psychology. Tim's perfect ten score on the horizontal bar during the team event clinched the U.S. team victory. Tim also won a bronze medal for his performance on the pommel horse, his favorite apparatus. The year 1984 was a gymnastic triumph for Tim, as he added three National Collegiate Athletic Association (NCAA) championships to his Olympic honors for his performances on the pommel horse, rings, and parallel bars. Then he celebrated 1985 by winning the American Cup men's all-around championship. His teammates call him "the Raging Bull" because of his intensity during practice.

Charles Shields, Tim's grandfather, showed perhaps the most patriotic response to the men's team gold medal. While watching the Olympics on television, Mr. Shields became so overwhelmed by Tim's perfect ten score that he started crying and ran outside in the middle of the night

Peter Vidmar performing on the side horse during team competition. His perfect ten score helped the U.S. take the lead midway through the Olympic competition.

to raise an American flag. He said later, "I was so thrilled that I had to tell everyone who went by that something had happened."

MITCH GAYLORD
Mitch Gaylord's popularity in the field of gymnastics comes from his interest in original stunts. A twenty-three-year-old native of California, Mitch lives in Van Nuys, and, like Tim Daggett, is a UCLA collegiate gymnast, while he majors in history. At the Los Angeles Games, besides his team gold medal, Mitch added a silver medal to his collection by tying China's Li Ning, Japan's Koji Gushiken and Shinji Morisue for second place on the vault. He then won two bronze medals for his performances on the rings and the parallel bars. A two-time winner of the United States National Men's Championship (1983 and 1984), Mitch Gaylord has been a member of the American men's gymnastic team for five years. Because of Mitch's handsome movie-star looks, Jim Hartung calls him "Hollywood Mitch."

Today Mitch is perhaps most well known for his original stunt, the "Gaylord II." Anyone who has seen him perform his trick is amazed to learn that Mitch used to be afraid of the horizontal bar. When he was fourteen, he used to hide whenever his coach gave instructions on the high bar. In the Gaylord II, a release move from the horizontal bar, Mitch performs a flyaway backflip with a half-twist, then recatches the bar in an undergrip, all in .81 second, a blink of an eye. "But when you're up there," Mitch says, "it feels like forever. When I was a little kid, I fell off a bridge into water. As I fell, I tried to breathe and couldn't, because all the air was in me. That's how I feel when I'm falling toward the bar. All the air is in me."

During the men's team event finals, Mitch Gaylord demonstrated the new gymnast attitude of playing for the team first. When his turn came up on the horizontal bar, the Chinese gymnasts were leading the United States by only

Mitch Gaylord on the horizontal bar, the apparatus he has come to dominate

(22)

.6 of a point. Mitch had to choose between performing a less risky stunt, and thereby scoring high enough to keep the United States in the running for the gold medal, or executing his Gaylord II which, if he nailed, would assure an American team victory.

Abie Grossfeld, coach of the U.S. men's gymnastic Olympic team, hesitated. "I knew how badly he wanted it. How long he'd worked on it." Against the coach's better judgment, he gave Mitch the green light. Mitch scored a 9.95, and the rest is history. Even the second-place Chinese would probably admit that Mitch's Gaylord II is a mind-boggling feat for someone who used to cringe every time he saw a horizontal bar.

BART CONNER

Born in Chicago, Illinois, Bart Conner now lives in Norman, Oklahoma. At twenty-six he is the oldest team member. Jim Hartung calls him "The Veteran." Bart graduated from the University of Oklahoma with a degree in journalism, and he is a public relations consultant when not performing awesome gymnastics, especially on the parallel bars, his specialty. Bart won the gold medal on this apparatus in the individual events competition at the 1984 Olympics.

As the publicity spokesperson for the men's team, Bart gives many interviews explaining why gymnastics is a healthy as well as exciting sport.

His gymnastic career illustrates his dedication to the sport and his drive to keep performing in spite of obstacles. In 1983 Bart underwent bicep surgery on his left elbow. The surgeon said Bart would need a year to recuperate. He ignored the surgeon and commuted to Las Vegas, Nevada, for physical therapy. Bart Conner wanted to make the 1984 Olympic team so much that when he missed the first of the two qualifying trials in May because of the surgery, he petitioned the United States Gymnastic Federation (USGF). This group is the governing organization of all U.S. gymnastics meets. Conner needed to see if

*Bart Conner in perfect
form during his
floor exercises routine*

they would let him qualify by using only his total score in the second Olympic trials, held in Jacksonville, Florida. With the USGF's approval, Bart and his physical therapist, who holds a master's degree in mathematics, calculated how many points Bart needed to score in each event to make the team. That way, Bart could conserve his energy on the routines in which he did not need to score as high. When the points were totaled, Bart Conner was in.

A three-time Olympic gymnastic team member, Bart is the person who most encouraged the American men gymnasts to change their competing attitude to one of playing to win. Thus the men's winning momentum, fueled by Bart Conner's pep talks, reached a peak at the Los Angeles Games. As he explained, "First our whole intention was to get ahead of the Japanese for the first time, and we'd give China as much of a scare as we could. . . . Then another thought popped up. Why not take the lead and get the best rotation. . . ?" (The leading team starts on floor exercises, the most physically demanding, and finishes on the pommel horse; the second-place team rotates in the opposite direction, finishing on floor exercises when their endurance is less strong.) That plan was "a far cry from the 1976 Olympics, when we weren't contending at all, when just one guy pulled off a medal, the first in forty-four years. It was regarded as a miracle, a fluke, hardly a change in gymnastic momentum."

After the 1984 Olympics, when the United States men gymnasts won the team championship, even their coach, Abie Grossfeld, said, "No one who knows gymnastics thought we'd beat the Chinese. I never thought I'd see this in my lifetime."

SCOTT JOHNSON

Originally from Cincinnati, Ohio, Scott Johnson, twenty-three, graduated from the University of Nebraska with a degree in public health. Although his favorite event is the rings, Scott may be the best in floor exercises. His teammates say he is well known for his Tarzan whoops during practice. They call him "the Good Humor Man," as he keeps everyone laughing. James Hartung says, "When everybody is so intense and our lives are on the line in these meets, it's nice to have somebody like Scott to help keep you relaxed."

The winning team: (left to right)
Tim Daggett, Scott Johnson,
Mitch Gaylord, Jim Hartung,
Peter Vidmar, and Bart Conner.

JAMES HARTUNG

James Hartung, twenty-four, is from Omaha, Nebraska. In 1983 he graduated from the University of Nebraska with a degree in business. James began his gymnastic career when he was twelve years old and has been on the U.S. men's gymnastic team for seven years. His teammates call him "the Philosopher," as he thinks of names for his teammates after "long deliberation" concerning their personalities.

The American men gymnasts felt deep emotion as they stood on the podium to receive their team gold medals. Peter Vidmar, tears rolling down his cheeks, declared, "The men's gymnastic team has become a new world power for years to come." Bart Conner added, "You grow up thinking, 'Wouldn't it be great to be in the finals of the Olympic trials?' Then you start thinking, 'Wouldn't it be great to be in the Olympics?' But you never think, 'Wouldn't it be great to be a gold medal winner?' Who could ask for anything more?"

For a gymnastic team that had not won an Olympic medal since 1932, when Indian club swinging was a major event, the United States men's grand total of eight medals, three of them gold, adds up to a great change in American gymnastics, and that is no fluke at all.

THE
MAKING
OF A
NEW
GYMNAST

Gymnastics is different from any other sport in that athletes rotate from one apparatus to another, performing stunts on each which have few related skills or movements. For example, a male gymnast does leg-lifting circle swings up and around the entire 64-inch (162.56-cm) length of the pommel horse, supporting his entire body weight with his hands. His dismount is usually from a handstand; yet in preparing a stunt for the horizontal bar, he must swing in giant circles around the bar without stopping, while he performs release moves involving somersaulting acrobatics before recatching the bar. Men usually end horizontal bar routines swinging fast around the bar until gaining enough momentum to dismount with a double somersault, or some other awesome stunt, and they must land with both feet hitting the mat at the same time.

Women experience the same challenge to master unrelated skills. For instance, while performing on the balance beam, they must possess extraordinary precision in order to flip, cartwheel, and handstand on a board barely 4 inches (10 cm) wide. At the same time, they must prepare floor exercise routines on the regulation 40-by-40-foot (12-by-12-m) mat, which involve mastering superior aerial acrobatic skills combined with the graceful ballet movements required for the dance portion of floor exercises. A woman has no time to see how close to the edge of the mat she will land out of a double-back somersault. She must learn to feel her space limits, since a step off the mat is a .15 point penalty.

IMPROVED EQUIPMENT

Today's new gymnasts have the advantage of perfecting their difficult and varied skills on new and improved equipment.

When gymnastics began centuries ago in ancient Greece, the sport was mainly track and field events. In the late nineteenth century, J. L. Jahn, a German gymnastics coach, invented the rings, the pommel horse, and the parallel bars, and changed gymnastics into the sport as we know it today.

The next gymnastic equipment renovation is credited to the Russian gymnast Olga Korbut. She asked that padding be placed on and underneath the balance beam. Since Olga was the first gymnast to perform daring stunts on the beam, such added comfort and safety for the gymnast had never been needed, or thought of, before. Today, thick padding mounted on springs is placed under every apparatus and functions like a launch pad, propelling gymnasts higher than ever during floor exercises and cushioning their landings from the equipment.

For men, wooden dowels have been invented, which they insert into their leather handgrips. The dowels provide a lock-grip on the horizontal and parallel bars, allowing them to swing in ever faster circles to perform release moves with less chance of losing their grip on the bars.

A special safety device has been invented for beginning women gymnasts on the balance beam, considered the most difficult apparatus in gymnastics. A hydraulic lifting platform can be attached to the bottom of the beam. As the gymnast progresses in skill, the coach raises the hydraulic platform accordingly. The platform is similar to the safety net used by trapeze artists: if the woman falls, she lands on the platform, instead of falling 4 feet (1.2 m) down to the floor.

*Tracee Talavera
displays new gymnast
dazzle as she flips
high above the
balance beam.*

THE "WOW" FACTOR Until the new gymnasts rejuvenated the sport into one of colossal, show-stopping routines, gymnastics had been called "the ballet of sports." Since 1896, when the first modern Olympics were held in Athens, Greece, gymnasts focused their performances on the grace and poise of ballet movements. Tumbling stunts were secondary to keeping their toes pointed and their arms and legs extended in beautiful ballet glides and turns across the floor. In addition, they performed routine, nonperilous acrobatics, which kept perfect tens unscored and the audience yawning.

The new gymnasts have turned "Ballet Gymnastics" into "Power Gymnastics" by focusing their performances on original and thrilling acrobatic stunts. New gymnasts possess incredible strength, body flexibility, unwavering concentration, and superior endurance. While their toes are still pointed, and they have retained the graceful style of the sport, new gymnasts strive to create a "Wow" factor in their routines, which judges look for in scoring each athlete's performance. Judges call this wow factor "ROV," meaning risk, originality, and virtuosity.

Mitch Gaylord defines ROV as the *spectacle*, saying, "Today's gymnasts go for the big trick, the 'killer move,' that leaves judges and spectators alike staring wide-eyed and openmouthed. . . . The judges must say to themselves, 'This is awesome. He's doing something nobody else is doing. If he nails it, he has to win.' "

Today's gymnasts do not ask themselves, Can this new stunt be done? but rather, How am I going to master it? Thus, with triple scoops of ROV packed into each routine, the new gymnasts have changed a mild-mannered tumbling event, attended by a dedicated few, into an international stunt race, in which each gymnast tries to outperform the other. Competitive gymnastics now rivals track and field as the event for which sports fans beat a path to

Li Ning wowed judges and spectators alike with his exciting performance during floor exercises competition.

the ticket window. This acrobatic stunt race has knocked down the fortress of traditional gymnastics, eliminating forever the tame format and the "ballet barrier" that kept many athletes from participating in the sport.

It is the new gymnasts' mastery of original, gravity-defying routines, involving unrelated and difficult skills, that has made today's "New Gymnastics" the ultimate thrill for spectators, and the unparalleled challenge for athletes.

SPECIALIZATION By specializing on the apparatus they like best, modern gymnasts have added a new feature to their race to outperform each other. Just as physicians specialize in different areas of medicine, such as children's illnesses or broken bones, so the new breed of gymnast specializes in creating a three-dimensional, electrifying routine for a specific apparatus. Often the gymnast becomes so famous for his or her stunt, that each time he or she appears in a meet or a gymnastic exhibition, the audience awaits in eager anticipation to see the gymnast perform the routine. After the Los Angeles Games, the United States Olympic gymnastic teams went on a national exhibition tour. The crowd burst into wild applause the moment Mitch Gaylord walked into the arena and the announcer mentioned the Gaylord II.

SELF-CONFIDENCE In order to score high points under the intense pressure of international competition, new gymnasts have developed supreme self-confidence in their abilities to execute perilous stunts. A new gymnastic attitude of total commitment to the sport runs parallel with belief in his or her talent. They have patience, determination, and endurance to practice each original stunt one step at a time. When the trick is mastered, in spite of the keen talent of the opponents, the gymnast feels confident in his or her ability to execute risky backflips on the balance beam, or triple somersaults off the rings.

Mary Lou's Retton Vault contains thousands of tiny movements, each one crucial to the success of the entire stunt. For Mary Lou, learning this vault may have involved jumping off the springboard at the end of the vaulting runway hundreds of times until she reached the necessary height and momentum to leap over the horse into her layout twists and back somersaults while still in the air.

(36)

Such repetitious practice for hours each day has made some talented young gymnasts give up, as they lack the patience to persevere. A true new gymnast, however, is entirely dedicated to gymnastics. As one coach put it, "Training is the name of the game."

TEAMWORK Just as baseball coaches prepare a batting order, so gymnastics coaches make up a performing order that depends upon the gymnast's commitment to putting the team's chances of winning before his or hers. Usually the weakest gymnast on the team performs first. The strategy is that if the first athlete does well, his or her score serves as a base from which the more skilled gymnasts on the team may receive higher scores—judges usually score a progression of less to more skilled athletes with higher and higher scores.

Sometimes a coach will reverse the performing order and put the best gymnast first. This strategy calls for a sacrifice play by the more skilled athlete, as most gymnasts prefer to perform last, when chances of receiving higher scores are more likely, especially of scoring perfect tens.

A "playing for the team" attitude was expressed by Peter Vidmar when he lost the gold medal in the men's all-around event by .025 of a point: "You could ask me to switch the team gold for this [the all-around championship], and I wouldn't do it. What we did the other night is still the greatest moment in American gymnastic history."

NEW IMAGES In addition to new, outward performance images, the new gymnasts have put on modern images of appearance. No longer do women gymnasts feel they have to stay extra slim in order to be graceful. Mary Lou Retton has probably done more to influence this new attitude of physical fitness than any other woman gymnast. Her stocky legs and muscular body build, which she calls "chunky," give her the power to run fast and leap high and do not keep her from performing gracefully. Mary Lou is a first-rate gymnast in the floor exercise, where a poised ballet style alternates with acrobatics. Her pixie hairdo has also broken tradition. Previous women gymnasts, in keeping with the traditional ballerina image, wore their hair in long ponytails or braids.

Inspired by Mary Lou's gymnastic triumphs, many gymnasts are copying her pixie look.

To round out her modern appearance, Mary Lou Retton has also perfected a unique style of carrying herself from apparatus to apparatus. She has eliminated the delicate footsteps of former gymnasts, which resembled tiptoeing upon a floor mat made of eggshells, and substituted it with the "Mary Lou Strut." Her shoulders rolling and her neck muscles flexing like a linebacker for the Dallas Cowboys, she moves across the floor in her trademark, a pigeon-toed saunter. Her family used to tease her about her stocky build. Mary Lou just grinned and said, "That's okay. I may not be whippy, but I've got all that power." Today she adds, "The other gymnasts walk like ballerinas just for show, to make us look classier than we really are. Ordinarily we all walk like little bitty football players."

A new image is "in" for men gymnasts as well. Their more elaborate stunts are the reason their bodies have developed into the muscular physiques of other "he-man" athletes. No longer is gymnastics considered a sport mainly for women, with male gymnasts pushed into the background. The men have moved into the spotlight, and are thrilling fans with a new kind of performance style—acrobatic entertainment. They have developed new techniques which emphasize relating to the audience.

Thus Peter Vidmar pauses atop the parallel bars after a risky maneuver to grin at the cheering crowd, or Mitch Gaylord perfectly executes his Gaylord II, then sighs in relief and wipes his forehead, smiling his agreement with the gasping audience. As a result, the men's names, like many of the women's, are becoming household words, and increasing numbers of boys are enrolling in gymnastic classes, wanting to be just like Bart Conner or Mitch Gaylord.

Ninety-five pounds of solid muscle and determination, Mary Lou exemplifies the new look of today's power gymmasts.

CELEBRITY
STATUS
The new gymnasts spend extra energy to perform incredible body contortions in a crowd-pleasing style. Even when executing a routine somersault, today's gymnasts sparkle with charisma. A striking side effect has happened. The new gymnasts have become celebrities, given the same star status as popular music groups or movie stars.

Fans make banners with Mary Lou Retton's name printed on them, or wave and shout to their favorite gymnast from the stands. Droves of young people wait at stadium exits for the chance to get a gymnast's autograph. Once, when Mary Lou had her hair cut, girls scrambled to grab strands of her shorn locks as souvenirs. The new gymnasts receive thousands of pieces of fan mail, and wherever they go people recognize them. Previously, gold medal gymnasts could eat at restaurants, attend plays, or simply walk down the street and blend in with other young people. Today, that kind of personal privacy has disappeared for them, as the near hysteria formerly reserved for movie and rock stars occurs around the new gymnasts whenever one person recognizes them and shouts their names.

Tim Daggett is surprised by his sudden fame. "Everywhere we go," he says, "the people go absolutely nuts. I can't believe it. I did a little exhibition in . . . a tiny town, and with hardly any advance notice, four thousand people showed up. Four years ago, you couldn't have done that with the entire Olympic team."

Mary Lou Retton, however, likes to watch the audience's reactions when she performs. "I like all the exposure," she says. "I think it's neat . . . all athletes deserve it for all the hard work they put in . . . and that podium . . . those medals . . . it's what you work for. What a great feeling . . . ."

New celebrities Mitch Gaylord and Mary Lou Retton meet an old pro, Bob Hope, at a party hosted by the U.S. Olympic Committee in Los Angeles.

(40)

As part of their celebrity status, the United States Olympic gymnastic teams tour the country staging acrobatic exhibitions. In November 1984 the American gymnasts returned to Pauley Pavilion, the scene of their Olympic triumph, and presented "American Gymnasts, Part II," while 11,528 roaring fans gave them a standing ovation just for parading around the arena. Girls screamed for Mitch Gaylord with the same wild enthusiasm teen-age girls showered on singer Elvis Presley in the 1950s.

In an exhibition, there is no competition, and as a result, no pressure to perform without faults. The gymnasts give a more personalized, relaxed show. Scott Johnson steadies the ring cords with his toes—a big "no-no" in real competition. The men's team puts on a gymnastic comedy routine, pretending to outdo each other in dismounts from the parallel bars. While Bart Conner swings into a handstand, preparing to dismount, the other team members run underneath the bars to distract Bart; while James Hartung whirls around the bars, the team chalks an *X* on the mat, marking the spot where to land; and Mitch Gaylord executes the apparent winning double back somersault dismount when the men pull the mat out from under him.

About the change in tempo and mood during exhibitions, Peter Vidmar says, "It's fun to relax mentally," and Mitch Gaylord notes, "This is a blast. This is definitely not boring."

LIFE-STYLE Gymnastic training for international competition is a full-time job. Thus, if a particular coach's gymnastic program is in another city, many teen-aged gymnasts live far away from home today. This means leaving families and friends to spend their teen-age years living in a dormitory, or with a substitute family, as Mary Lou Retton did. Some gymnasts feel that living away from home helps them become independent decision makers, responsible for their choices. Others are concerned about having to postpone finishing high school or take correspondence courses to graduate with their class. Mary Lou Retton has chosen this latter route to a high school diploma. Regarding the time spent practicing gymnastics rather than spent living a traditional teen-ager's life, most gymnasts feel as Mary Lou Retton that "it's a trade-off. I really miss the proms and going to the games, and my classmates and all, but I've got this thing I've got to do first. First I've got to win."

Until the 1984 Olympics, European gymnasts shared the gold medal glory. Now the American gymnasts have turned the tide of gymnastic championships rolling toward the shores of the United States for the first time in gymnastic history. As the "veteran" United States team member, Bart Conner expresses the feelings of the American gymnasts when he says, "I've been a part of gymnastics in America when we weren't any good at all. I remember in 1976 we were in awe of the Russians and the Chinese. Back then, the biggest thing was just making the team. We were the best of the worst. To be a part of it now, when we come to this moment, when we finally pull it off . . . I'm so happy I stayed around to be a part of this."

4

PRESENTING THE NEW GYMNASTS: THE WOMEN

The night before the women's Olympic gymnastic team event finals, Mary Lou Retton lay in bed at the Olympic Village fantasizing about winning gold medals.

"I see myself hitting all my routines," she said of her nightly daydreams, "doing everything perfectly. I imagine all the moves and go through them with the image in my mind."

Mary Lou Retton's Olympic medal fantasy came true the next day, when the United States women's gymnastic team won the silver medal in the team competition. While it was not the gold medal, their victory was nevertheless historic. The United States women had won the first American Olympic gymnastic medal *ever*, and the first U.S. team medal in international competition.

ENTER THE WOMEN GYMNASTS: BEGINNING STRIDES

Women gymnasts broke the "Men Only" rule of international gymnastic competition when they were first permitted to enter Olympic gymnastics at the 1928 Games in Amsterdam, Holland. Yet they were allowed to compete only in combined team exercises. Not until 1952, at the Helsinki, Finland, Olympics, were women finally allowed to compete in the four gymnastic events still used in women's international gymnastic competition: the balance beam, the uneven parallel bars, the vault, and the floor exercises.

The Helsinki Games also marked the first appearance of the Soviet Union in Olympic competition, and Russia has dominated gymnastic championships ever since. Maria Gorokhovskaya won the all-around championship that year, and both the Soviet men's and women's team won

(47)

the combined team events championship. From 1956 until 1960, Soviet gymnast Larissa Latynina held the women's all-around title.

Czechoslavakian gymnast Vera Caslavska wrested the all-around title from Larissa Latynina, and held onto it through the 1968 Olympics in Mexico City, when she retired. Vera Caslavska is remembered for her floor exercise at those Olympics, when she impressed spectators and judges by performing to the music of "The Mexican Hat Dance." She is also recorded as the gymnast who has won more medals, eighteen in all, than any other athlete, man or woman, in any Olympic event. Vera Caslavska ranks also as the first gymnast to put sparkle into her performance, and thus she paved the way for a seventeen-year-old Russian gymnast to knock traditional gymnastics out of the ball park, and set the sport flaming with a new style.

OLGA KORBUT   At the Munich, Germany, Olympics of 1972, Olga Korbut, wearing her soon-to-be trademark pigtails, exploded onto the gymnastic scene. While traditional women gymnasts wore serious ballerina type expressions, and performed with rigid movements, making them appear more like computerized robots than human beings with feelings, Olga Korbut did something no other gymnast had ever done before—she smiled at the audience. The crowd was overwhelmed by her acknowledgment of their presence. Then Olga further thrilled the spectators and shocked judges by executing a back somersault off the balance beam. Although she was not the best gymnast on the Soviet team, finishing seventh in the all-around competition, Olga Korbut's bubbling personality and charm made the audience literally fall in love with her. Spectators further swept her into their hearts when she fell off the uneven

Olga Korbut gave a spectacular performance on the balance beam at the 1972 Olympics in Munich.

(48)

parallel bars during the finals of the women's all-around, and sat on a bench and cried in front of millions. A woman in the audience climbed over the barrier and handed Olga a bouquet of flowers, and fifteen thousand spectators—plus millions more watching their televisions at home—sympathized with Olga. She found herself elevated to a star status never before given to a woman gymnast.

Olga Korbut fan clubs were formed and teen-agers the world over wore "Olga Korbut Fan Club T-Shirts," wrote her fan letters, some addressed simply, "To Olga," and joined gymnastics clubs, wanting to be just like her.

Bela Karolyi remembers Olga Korbut as "the first gymnast to have an exciting style, besides the difficult stunts . . . she gave the expression of joy to the performer."

When Olga executed her famous back somersault and recatch off the uneven parallel bars, the news commentator George Madux shouted, "Oh . . . My . . . Wow!" His co-commentator asked if that trick had ever been done before. George Madux answered, "Not by any human."

NADIA COMANECI   A new gymnastic star was born at the 1976 Olympics in Montreal, Canada. Fourteen-year-old Nadia Comaneci of Romania executed even more daring stunts than Olga. Nadia performed with sheer excellence, although she rarely smiled or seemed aware of the audience's presence. She avoided the spotlight, shunning publicity. Therefore, no one knew much about her, which seemed to surround her with an aura of mystery. This "Nadia Mystique" bewitched crowds as much as Olga Korbut had with her bouncy personality.

Her original coach, Bela Karolyi, discovered Nadia when he happened to see her pretending to be a gymnast during recess in an elementary school. He recognized her

Nadia Comaneci scored perfect 10s across the board for her performances on the beam and the uneven bars at the 1976 Olympics in Montreal.

potential to become a star, and enrolled her in his training program. Nadia Comaneci was six years old.

A sports critic once wrote that Nadia's stunts seemed impossible from a "biomechanical viewpoint." An Olympic official judged her stunts so dangerous that he requested them banned from international competition. Olympic coach Don Peters says, "Nadia was in a class by herself. . . . She was head and shoulders above the rest, and for that she was appreciated."

Nadia was the first gymnast to score a perfect ten, and in Montreal she won the all-around championship, plus two gold medals for her performances on the balance beam and the uneven parallel bars.

At the 1980 Moscow Olympics, Nadia lost the all-around gold medal when judges from Poland and the Soviet Union gave her 9.85 on her balance beam performance, just low enough to give Russian gymnast Yelena Davydova the title. Nadia tied for the silver, and won two gold medals for the balance beam and floor exercises. These would be the last medals she would ever win.

Nadia intended to enter the 1984 Olympics, and had started training with the Romanian coach. However, six weeks before the Los Angeles Games, a Romanian official made a puzzling announcement. Nadia would not be coming to the 1984 Olympics as a gymnastic team member. She had retired from gymnastic competition.

Nadia Comaneci was twenty-two years old.

ECATERINA SZABO AND THE ROMANIAN NEW GYMNASTS

Seventeen-year-old Ecaterina Szabo is being promoted as the next Nadia Comaneci. She is a self-confident, aggressive gymnast, noted for her faultless performances and for her smooth movements in joining several stunts into one acrobatic routine. Ecaterina excites spectators with her four backward handsprings on the balance beam—two

Ecaterina Szabo took several gold medals in individual events and gave Mary Lou stiff competition for the all-around gold medal.

more than any other gymnast has attempted. She is considered the world champion tumbler in floor exercises, having placed third in the 1983 World Championships, behind the Soviet Union's star gymnast, Natalia Yurchenko. Szabo won the gold medal for floor exercises in the 1984 Olympics, tied for the gold on the balance beam with Simona Pauca, and took the gold medal on the vault.

Ecaterina's teammates, Lavinia Agache, Simona Pauca, and Laura Cutina, took their inspiration from Nadia Comaneci as well. However, as new gymnasts, they strive to outperform their mentor. When Lavinia was asked if she wanted to be as good as Nadia, she answered, "Yes. I want to be better."

JULIANNE MCNAMARA AND THE AMERICAN NEW GYMNASTS

Along with teammate Mary Lou Retton, Julianne McNamara lives in Houston, Texas, where she trains with Bela Karolyi. In addition to her silver medal for the team competition in the 1984 Olympics, Julianne also won a silver medal for her performance on the floor exercises, and tied with China's Ma Yanhonjg for the gold medal on the uneven parallel bars. She and Ma are the two top gymnasts on the uneven bars in the world. Julianne flies through her bar routine with a speed no other gymnast can muster. Ma Yanhonjg executes a series of recatches, including two using no hands.

When Julianne and Ma tied for the gold medal, Don Peters said, "They deserve to win. They've been competing against each other for years. They were both perfect."

Julianne's perfect performance, including a double backflip dismount, earned her the first ten ever scored by an American woman gymnast in international competition.

Eighteen-year-old Julianne McNamara is a self-disciplined student as well as a hardworking gymnast. She graduated from high school with a 3.95 average, out of a

Julianne McNamara's stunning routine on the uneven bars tied her for the gold medal with China's Ma Yanhonjg.

4-point system. Julianne hopes to have a career in either sports medicine or acting when she retires from gymnastics.

TRACEE
TALAVERA

Seventeen-year-old Tracee Talavera has studied gymnastics for eleven years. She placed first on the balance beam at the 1984 McDonald's Cup, and won the all-around championship at the 1984 USFG United States Classic Meet in Niagara Falls, New York.

DIANNE
DURHAM

Dianne started gymnastic lessons at age four, and won the Women's National Championship at age fifteen. At the 1984 McDonald's U.S.A. vs. the People's Republic of China Dual Meet in Honolulu, Dianne won the all-around competition. She, too, is a Bela Karolyi protegée, and lives in Houston.

KATHY
JOHNSON

When she was twelve, Kathy Johnson performed her first backflip off the baseball fence of her junior high school. Since then she has dreamed of winning an Olympic medal. For almost thirteen years she has overcome obstacles and injuries, striving to achieve her goal. A broken foot bone once kept her away from gymnastics for eight months, and she missed out on trying for an Olympic medal when the United States boycotted the Moscow Games in 1980.

On a Sunday night in 1984, in Los Angeles' Pauley Pavilion, Kathy performed an electrifying routine on the balance beam. Tears filled her eyes the instant her feet hit the mat. Kathy Johnson's goal, begun on the baseball fence, had come true. She had won her Olympic medal, even though it was a bronze.

"This makes it all worth it," she said. "I always tried to imagine what it would be like to win an Olympic medal . . . but you have to experience it." Then, tears streaming down her cheeks, Kathy Johnson announced her retirement from gymnastics.

Winning a bronze medal in the balance beam competition was a dream come true for Kathy Johnson.

(56)

Olga Korbut and Nadia Comaneci have left a legacy of popularized, modernized gymnastics, the impact of which is being felt more and more. It has been reported that in the ten years following Olga's debut, ten thousand gymnastics clubs opened in America to handle the increased enrollment, which skyrocketed from 15,000 gymnasts to 150,000. Practically every new gymnast today was somehow inspired by Olga or Nadia. Although these two women's routines seem old-fashioned compared to the new gymnasts' original stunts, a part of Olga's or Nadia's trend toward a more dramatic, athletic gymnastics remains inside each new gymnast's performance. In fact, if Olga and Nadia had not broken traditional gymnastic attitudes, many of today's exciting acrobatics would not have been created, and many new gymnasts, like Mary Lou Retton and Julianne McNamara, might not have entered gymnastics at all.

Mary Lou Retton, one of the new gymnasts inspired by Nadia Comaneci's legendary trend setting, says that to be a complete gymnast, "Someone should be able to sneak up and drag you out at midnight, and push you on some strange floor, and you should be able to do your entire routine sound asleep in your pajamas. *Without one mistake.* That's the secret. It's got to be a natural reaction."

Winners all, the bronze-winning Chinese team congratulates the American silver medalists as the gold-winning Romanian team looks on.

PRESENTING
THE
NEW
GYMNASTS:
THE
MEN

"We don't come to the Olympics just for gold medals. We come to rejoin the Olympic family. . . . We want to be able to come together with all people to compete in the Olympic spirit." Zhou Lifang, Deputy Chief, People's Republic of China, News Agency, 1984

The 1984 Olympics marked China's first participation in Olympic competition. Their athletes might not have come just to win gold medals, but win them they did—seven individual medals, including four gold, as well as a silver medal in the team competition, and a bronze medal in the all-around.

At the 1983 World Championships, the Chinese men's gymnastic team was crowned best in the world, beating the number one ranked Soviet Union.

LI NING Twenty-year-old Li Ning is considered one of the best male gymnasts in the world, along with the Soviet Union's Dmitri Belozerchev. Li first emerged as a top gymnast in 1982 at the World Cup Competition in Zagreb, Yugoslavia. He won six out of a possible seven gold medals in that meet, including the all-around championship.

Coaches and gymnasts like Li Ning, and admire his skill. When Peter Vidmar won the all-around competition at the American Cup Competition in New York, he turned his victory party into a celebration for Li, who had stumbled on the second day of the meet.

Li Ning has an exciting tumbling routine. Abie Grossfeld insists that Li clears 10 feet (3 m) during his backflips. Other gymnasts wonder at Li's seemingly continual good spir-

its. They say he never stops smiling, and that there is no other gymnast more humble. He also has a good sense of humor. When asked if there was anything he would like to improve upon before the Los Angeles Games began, Li said, "I'm not strong enough. I am not as strong as Mitch Gaylord." He smiled, a mischievous twinkle in his eyes. "Well, maybe, but I'm not as strong as his brother." Li referred to Mitch's brother and private coach, Chuck, a former gymnast.

Abie Grossfeld responded that "Li was just being humble. He's stronger than anybody. He's just like a little boy. . . . He's always been like that."

Li Ning, like other new gymnasts, is a determined athlete. Often the results of his determination surprise people, as part of his sincere modesty is a reluctance to boast of his accomplishments. Months before the 1984 Olympics, Li told his friends on the United States men's gymnastic team that he intended to master English in time for the Games in Los Angeles. The American men laughed. English is one of the most difficult languages to learn for someone who was not born in a country where English is the primary language. The American gymnasts thought no more about Li's statement until much later, when they attended a gymnastic function. The United States gymnasts stood talking in a group. Li approached them, and suddenly Mitch Gaylord sneezed. "God bless you," Li said, and grinned at the shocked expressions on the Americans' faces.

Always cheerful, when the Los Angeles Games ended, Li, still smiling, announced he was off to Disneyland.

THE SOVIET GYMNASTS
From 1952 until 1984, the Russian men gymnasts have won the team title every year, with the exception of the Japanese reigns in 1960 and 1964. The Soviet women held on to the team title until 1984.

China's Li Ning
shows perfect form
on the parallel bars.

VICTOR CHUKARIN

In the Helsinki Olympics of 1952, Victor Chukarin led the way for Russia's takeover of international gymnastic competition. Chukarin won the all-around title that year, and again in 1956, a remarkable feat, in that he was then thirty-five years old. He won two more gold medals, plus one silver, and one bronze, giving him eleven medals earned in two Olympics.

NIKOLAI ANDRIANOV

When the Russian men's team regained their top ranking from the Japanese, Nikolai Andrianov stole the all-around title from Japanese gymnast Sawao Kato, who had held the honor since 1968. Andrianov won three more gold medals for his performances on the floor exercises, vault, and rings. He is a contender for the title of greatest male gymnast of all time, having won a total of seven gold medals, five silver, and three bronzes in Olympic competitions, marking him as the male gymnast who has won the most medals in international competition.

ALEXANDER DITIATIN

Alexander Ditiatin is the only male gymnast to win Olympic medals in all eight categories. In 1980 he won gold medals for the team title, the all-around championship, and for his performance on the rings. He won a silver medal for the horizontal bar, vault, pommel horse, and parallel bars; and a bronze for his floor exercises. Alexander Ditiatin was the first male gymnast to score a perfect ten, which he received for his vault routine.

THE JAPANESE GYMNASTS

Masao Takemoto, having won five medals in two previous Olympics, led the Japanese men to their team victory in 1960. Takemoto was forty years old at the time, the oldest gymnast to win a gold medal in Olympic history.

Alexander Ditiatin performing at the World Gymnastics Championships in Houston in 1979. His agility on the rings won him a gold medal at the 1980 Olympics in Moscow.

(66)

In 1964 Japanese gymnast Yukio Endo captured the all-around title. However, he barely had time to polish it when Sawao Kato intercepted the all-around in 1968, and again in the 1972 Olympics.

MITSUO TSUKAHARA One of the most famous names in Japanese gymnastics is Mitsuo Tsukahara, inventor of the "Tsukahara." In 1976, during the finals of the team competition, he needed a 9.50 on the horizontal bar to lift Japan into first place. Tsukahara scored a 9.90, fitting the Japanese gymnasts firmly into the championship.

Japan is the country that has won the most men's team medals, five in all, compared to the Soviet Union's three.

KOJI GUSHIKEN In 1976, when the Soviet Union toppled Japan's number one gymnastic ranking, Koji Gushiken ranked as the thirteenth best Japanese gymnast. He kept striving to perfect his routines, however, and in the 1979 World Championships, he placed third in the all-around. A year later, Koji leaped into second place in the all-around, behind the Soviet Union's Dmitri Belozerchev.

Koji Gushiken, at twenty-seven years old, came to the Los Angeles Games intending to win medals. In 1980, when he had finally progressed in skill enough to qualify for the Moscow Olympics, Japan, along with the United States and other countries, boycotted the Games. Therefore Gushiken had to wait another four years to make his great showing.

"That is why I trained so hard for this," he said. "To win double gold."

Scoring a 9.90 or better in thirteen out of eighteen routines, Koji achieved his goal. He won the men's all-around gold medal, in addition to a gold medal on the rings, a silver medal on the vault, and a bronze medal on the horizontal bar, where Gushiken performs a full layout dismount.

Koji Gushiken in the floor
exercises competition
at the 1984 Olympics

Koji Gushiken practices the old-world tradition of concentrated elegance in performing each stunt. Yet he has the new gymnast attitudes of precision, determination, and perfection. Possessing also the new gymnast dedication to the sport, Koji arranged his work schedule in Japan so he could teach half a day at the Nippon College of Health and Physical Education in Tokyo, and practice gymnastics during the other half.

Like most gymnasts, Gushiken has had to overcome injuries. In 1975 he broke his ankle so badly he almost had to give up gymnastics. The following year he ruptured his Achilles' tendon. Yet with persevering spirit he said, "At my pace, I knew eventually a medal would come."

As he stood on the podium to receive his gold medal for the men's all-around championship, tears filled Koji Gushiken's eyes. After sixteen years of being a gymnast, he had not only qualified for his first Olympics but had also won the most coveted prize in gymnastic competition. As Koji sang the Japanese national anthem, perhaps he felt a special kinship with the sentiment expressed of maintaining the determination to survive and be present when other forces make trying again or going on seem impossible. For Koji Gushiken's life, up until that moment, had paralleled the words of his own national anthem.

Like the new women gymnasts, the new wave of men gymnasts continues to remodel the old gymnastic traditions with ingenious, incredible routines. They strive to push gymnastics further away from its origins as plain acrobatics and closer to the ultimate in a challenging, space-age competitive sport.

6

ON THE
BEAM:
NEW
GYMNASTS
IN THE
FUTURE

"Parents are calling from all over the country wanting to get their children started in the program. I couldn't begin to tell you how many calls we've had in the past few days." Bela Karolyi

The man who coached Mary Lou Retton and Julianne McNamara to eight Olympic medals in 1984 wasn't the only gymnastics instructor who was affected by the national captivation with gymnastics after the Los Angeles Olympics. The winning acrobatics of the new gymnasts sparked thousands of parents to dash out to enroll their children in gymnastics classes practically before the orchestra in Pauley Pavilion had finished playing the national anthem.

THE
GYMNASTIC
GOLD
RUSH

The new gymnasts triggered a gymnastic gold rush in which young people who used to dream of winning Olympic medals by jumping hurdles or nailing high dives now dream of going for the gold on balance beams, parallel bars, and vaulting horses. In less than two months after the 1984 Olympics, Bela Karolyi signed up six hundred new students in his gymnastic school in Houston, Texas. This was double his normal enrollment. And Gary Rafaloski, Mary Lou Retton's gymnastics coach during her early years, enrolled four hundred and fifty aspiring gymnasts into his Aerial Port Gym in Fairmont, West Virginia, and put three hundred more on a waiting list.

Some gymnastics coaches, such as Michael Cates, owner of Broadway Gymnastic School in Santa Monica, California, teach very young gymnasts. Mr. Cates enrolls children as young as a year and a half. He says, "Gym-

nastics is a fun and safe way for young children to help develop and strengthen their growing muscles. Even toddlers can master simple acrobatic exercises, such as somersaults or headstands on a well-padded floor mat. Gymnastics provides physical fitness for toddlers, and also gives these children a blast of a fun time."

With soaring numbers of young people wanting to take gymnastic lessons, but with classes across the country filled and waiting lists overflowing, a new concept has been suggested for the future to enable coaches to handle the sport's increasing popularity. This idea is a large gymnastic training facility, which would serve as a boarding school also. Thus the competing teen-age gymnast's dilemma of delaying his or her high school education, or taking correspondence courses while on a gymnastic team, would be solved.

FINDING A GOOD GYMNASTIC PROGRAM

Gymnastics is more than a sport in which athletes compete for gold medals on an apparatus. Gymnastics is a lifelong way to keep physically fit. The sport exercises every muscle in the body, making arms, legs, hips, and even the spine limber and strong. Many adults now take gymnastics classes as well. There are no requirements as to age, height, or weight to participate in the sport, and gymnastics doesn't depend on good weather for enthusiasts to participate.

There are, however, some dangers involved. Twisted wrists and ankles, sprains, pulled muscles, or broken bones may occur if certain safety measures are not available or followed. For this reason, it is wise to find a gymnastic training program with well-trained coaches and sturdy, well-maintained apparatus. Many gymnastics coaches are now taking college physical education courses to learn *how* to teach gymnastics, as well as *what* to teach.

Michael Cates, owner of the Broadway Gymnastic School, spots a young gymnast about to attempt his first somersault off the springboard trampoline.

Mr. Joe Fitz, a professional in sports medicine at St. Joseph Hospital in Fort Worth, Texas, suggests finding out how long the coach has taught gymnastics; how many injuries have occurred at his or her facility, and what kind; and getting opinions of others who have enrolled there. He especially cautions against choosing dance studios that offer gymnastics, as their instructors are most likely not sufficiently trained in gymnastics. As one coach said, "After every Olympics, dance studios start offering gymnastics . . . this is dangerous. We don't try to teach dancing in gymnastic class, after all."

In addition, Mr. Fitz recommends comparing different gymnastic schools to observe how young people are taught. Is there a spotter present at all times? A spotter is the coach, or the coach's assistant, who stands close to the student, helping him or her execute stunts, ready to catch the gymnast should he or she fall. Even Olympic gold medalists have spotters when not officially competing in a meet.

Mr. Fitz stresses that the best way to avoid injuries is to follow the number one safety precaution which professional gymnasts always observe: Never get up on any apparatus unless an instructor is watching.

FROM PRACTICE TO COMPETITION

New gymnastic students start at the Beginning Level, and advance to the Intermediate, Advanced, and Elite Level by passing a performance test, in which they must show mastery of each acrobatic maneuver taught at the lower level. The Elite Level has levels of its own, from IV to I, with I being the highest. Usually a gymnast must attain the Advanced Level before being on a team or competing against other local teams in meets called Intra-Gymnastic Meets.

Young gymnasts working on balance beam techniques at the Oregon Academy of Artistic Gymnastics in Eugene, Oregon

Seniors in high school may compete in an annual Seniors Meet, at which college scouts attend to offer some gymnasts full gymnastic college scholarships. Thus the gymnast obtains a college education while participating on the college gymnastic team.

Usually only Elite gymnasts compete in qualifying meets to be chosen for the United States gymnastic men's or women's teams. There are six members on each team.

GOING
FOR THE
GOLD:
INTERNATIONAL
MEETS

The United States Gymnastic Team competes in several international meets, the most famous of which are the World Championships, the Pan-American Games, the World University Games, and the Olympic Games, all held annually, except the Olympics, which are held every four years.

A gymnastics meet is really three separate events in one: the team championship, the individual all-around championship, and the individual apparatus championship.

THE
COMBINED
EVENTS
TEAM
CHAMPIONSHIP

Each team participates in compulsory and optional exercises on each apparatus. Compulsory exercises are prescribed, identical gymnastic stunts, such as a handstand on the rings, or a backflip on the floor exercises. Compulsories are established by the International Gymnastic Federation (IGF), the organization responsible for all international gymnastics meets and are changed every four years. Optional exercises are original routines performed by each gymnast. To determine the winning team, each gymnast's highest and lowest scores for each apparatus are eliminated, and the remaining two middle scores are averaged. Then each teams's top five averages are added together, and the highest scoring team wins.

THE
INDIVIDUAL
ALL-AROUND
CHAMPIONSHIP

The highest scoring thirty-six gymnasts in the team competition, with no more than three gymnasts from each country, compete in another round of compulsory and optional exercises.

The winner is determined by adding half the score of the gymnast in the team competition to his or her score in the all-around.

THE INDIVIDUAL APPARATUS OR EVENT CHAMPIONSHIP

The eight highest scoring gymnasts on each apparatus in the team competition, with no more than two gymnasts from each country competing on a single apparatus, enter the individual apparatus competition. The winners on each apparatus are determined by adding half the gymnast's score in the team competition *on that apparatus* to his or her score on the *same* apparatus in the individual events competition.

JUDGES AND SCORING

Four judges score each gymnast on a scale of 1 to 10, and subtract points for faults in .1 of a point deductions. For example, points may be deducted for failing to execute each compulsory exercise required for an apparatus; falling off the apparatus, which is an automatic .5 penalty; stepping out of bounds during the floor exercises, a .1 penalty; or not landing with both feet touching the mat at the same time, for which up to .20 of a point may be deducted.

RHYTHMIC GYMNASTICS

In the nineteenth century, Peter Ling of Sweden invented free floor exercises, which evolved into the sport of rhythmic gymnastics. Although the sport was recognized by the IGF in 1962, rhythmic gymnastics only made its official debut at the Olympics in 1984.

Rhythmic gymnastics is different from artistic gymnastics in that gymnasts perform *with* hand apparatus, rather than *upon* apparatus. This apparatus consists of wooden or plastic hoops, rubber balls, Indian clubs, and a 19.5-foot (59.4-m) long satin ribbon. Only women may compete in this sport, in which they perform modern dance and ballet routines set to music, while juggling, throwing, and twirling the apparatus. The trick is to keep the apparatus moving at all times. The skilled coordination involved is like rubbing your stomach in big, round circles with one hand, while patting the top of your head with the other.

The gymnastic Gold Rush shows no signs of slowing down. Therefore, future new gymnasts will face an even greater challenge in winning any kind of medals. These new gymnasts will have to be as totally committed to the sport as their heroes and heroines are today, stretching beyond their own outer limits of body contortions and endurance to create ever more original, spellbinding gymnastic routines.

When Olympic headlines fade into yesterday's news, the achievements of today's new gymnasts will be recorded in the history books of tomorrow. These athletes' historic feats, combined with their sheer joy in performance, will continue to inspire young gymnasts the world over.

As future new gymnasts practice tumbling in floor exercises, somersaulting across balance beams, and swinging around horizontal and parallel bars, somewhere a young boy may invent a thrilling new stunt. If his acrobatics are daring enough, his creation might be the next Gaylord II. And somewhere else a young girl may take her first leap over the vault. If she "flat *loves* flying like that," she might very well become the next Mary Lou Retton.